You[r] crowd [...] want o[...] desk with a pencil can stuffed with colorful critters.

Pig Topper

SIZE: 2½" x 3½"

MATERIALS:
   Pencil
   2" Pink Pom pom
   2" x 3" Light Pink foam
   2 Black 3mm half round beads for eyes
   Pink crayon
   Bright Pink Shiny fabric paint
   Fabri-Tac Glue

INSTRUCTIONS:
• Cut out legs, snout, and head from foam using patterns.
• Glue snout and eyes to face.
• Color cheeks and ear centers with crayon.
• Paint nostrils and hooves. Let dry.
• Glue the pom pom to the eraser end of the pencil.
• Glue legs and face to body.

Elephant Topper

SIZE: 3½" x 4"

MATERIALS:
   Pencil
   Pom poms (1 Gray 1½", 5 Gray ½")
   Felt (Gray, Pink)
   2 wiggle eyes 7mm
   6" Blue ⅛" wide ribbon
   Fabri-Tac Glue

INSTRUCTIONS:
• Glue the 1½" pom pom to the eraser end of the pencil.
• Glue the small Gray pom poms together end-to-end for a trunk.
• Glue trunk to bottom of large pom pom.
• Tie a ribbon bow around pencil, just below elephant.
• Cut ears from felt using pattern.
• Glue ears to back of head.
• Glue eyes in place.

Bear Topper

SIZE: 2½" x 3½"

MATERIALS:
   Pencil
   2" Tan Pom pom
   Foam (3" x 4" Tan, ½" Brown)
   2 Black 3mm half round beads for eyes
   Black fine tip marker, Brown Shiny fabric paint
   Fabri-Tac Glue

INSTRUCTIONS:
• Cut out bear and muzzle from Tan foam using patterns.
• Cut out nose from Brown foam.
• Glue muzzle, nose and eyes to face.
• Draw whisker dots and mouth line on muzzle with a marker.
• Paint ear centers and paw pads. Let dry.
• Glue the pom pom to the eraser end of the pencil.
• Glue the foam body to back of pom pom.

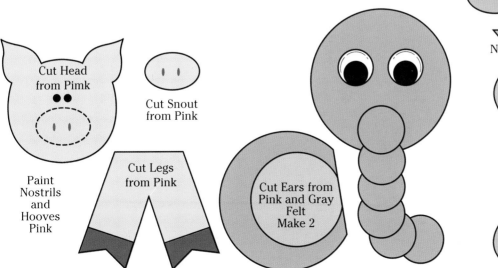

Cut Head from Pimk

Cut Snout from Pink

Paint Nostrils and Hooves Pink

Cut Legs from Pink

Cut Ears from Pink and Gray Felt Make 2

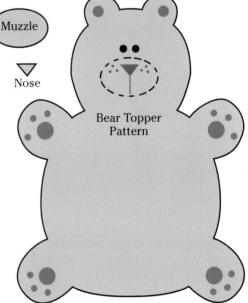

Muzzle

Nose

Bear Topper Pattern

Fish Topper

SIZE: 2½" x 3½"

MATERIALS:
Pencil
2 Lime Green 2" pom poms
3½" x 3½" Yellow foam
Fabric paint (Mint Sparkle, Black Shiny)
Fabri-Tac Glue

INSTRUCTIONS:
• Cut out face, fins, and tail from foam using patterns.
• Paint lines on fins, tail and eyes. with Mint paint. Let dry.
• Dot eyes with Black. Let dry.
• Sandwich and glue the head, tail and top fin between the two pom poms.
• Glue the pom poms to the eraser end of the pencil.
• Glue side fins to body.

Fish Patterns

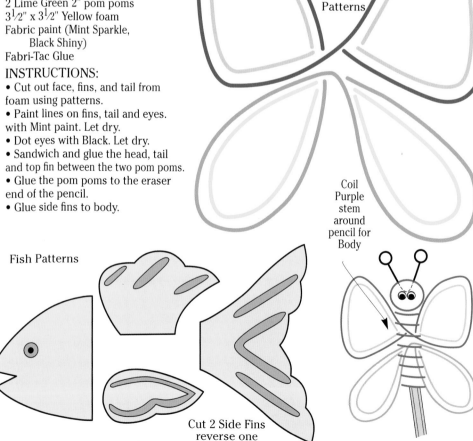

Cut 2 Side Fins reverse one

Top and Bottom Butterfly Wings Patterns

Coil Purple stem around pencil for Body

Top your favorite pencil with a friendly critter.

Butterfly Topper

SIZE: 3½" x 4"

MATERIALS:
Pencil
Chenille stems (Purple, Dark Pink, Turquoise, Light Blue, Hot Pink, Yellow, Black)
Pom poms (1 Purple ½", 2 Black ¼")
2 wiggle eyes 5mm
Fabri-Tac Glue

INSTRUCTIONS:
• Coil Purple stem around top of pencil.
• Glue Purple pom pom to top as head.
• Cut 2" piece of Black stem, fold into a V, and glue to head.
• Glue Black pom poms to antennae and 2 eyes to face.
• Wrap Pink stem to form the 2 top wings.
• Wrap Turquoise stem to form the 2 bottom wings.
• Cut two 4" pieces of Blue stem and glue to inside of Pink wings.
• Cut two 3" pieces of Yellow stem and glue to inside of Turquoise wings.
• Glue wings to back of Purple body.

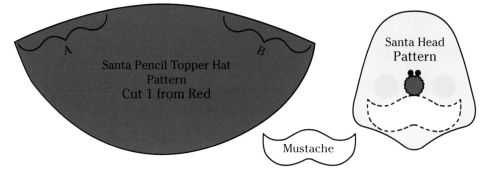

Santa Pencil Topper Hat Pattern
Cut 1 from Red

A   B

Santa Head Pattern

Mustache

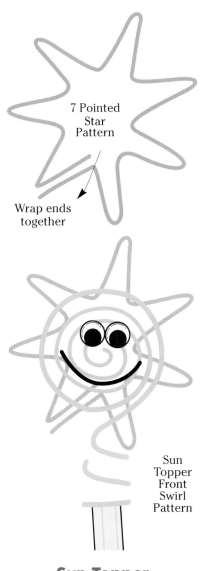

7 Pointed Star Pattern

Wrap ends together

Sun Topper Front Swirl Pattern

Sun Topper

Brighten your day with a smiling, sunny pencil topper.

SIZE: 2½" x 2½"

MATERIALS:
Pencil
Chenille stems (Yellow, Light Orange)
2 wiggle eyes 7mm
Black cord
Fabri-Tac Glue

INSTRUCTIONS:
• Spiral Yellow stem leaving 3" straight on end.
• Coil end around pencil.
• Zigzag Orange stem forming 7 points.
• Wrap ends together forming star shape.
• Glue to back of Yellow spiral.
• Glue eyes to face.
• Cut 1" of cord and glue as mouth.

Santa Topper

SIZE: 2½" x 3½"

MATERIALS:
Pencil
Pom poms (White 2", White ½", Red 5mm)
Foam (2" x 3½" Red, 2" x 2" Peach, ½" x 1½" White)
2 Black 3mm half round beads for eyes
Red crayon
White Shiny fabric paint
Fabri-Tac Glue

INSTRUCTIONS:
• Cut out hat, face, and mustache from foam using patterns.
• Color cheeks with crayon.
• Glue the 2" White pom pom to the eraser end of the pencil.
• Glue eyes, nose and mustache to face.
• Roll hat into a cone shape and glue A to B.
• Paint squiggle lines around bottom of hat; let dry. Glue ½" White pom pom to top of hat. Glue face and hat to head.

Cat Topper

SIZE: 2½" x 2½"

MATERIALS:
Pencil
1 Tan 2" pom pom
2½" x 3½" Tan foam
Brown fine tip marker
2 Black 3mm half round beads for eyes
Pale Peach Shiny fabric paint
Fabri-Tac Glue

INSTRUCTIONS:
• Cut out face, legs and tail from foam using patterns.
• Paint ear centers and nose triangle on face. Let dry.
• Draw toe lines, whiskers, whisker dots and mouth with marker.
• Glue eyes to face.
• Glue the pom pom to the eraser end of the pencil.
• Glue face, tail and paws to pom pom.

Bee Topper

SIZE: 2½" x 3"

MATERIALS:
Pencil
Pom poms (Yellow 2", Black ¾")
Black foam (3" x 3" and ½" x 3½")
4" x 5½" White tulle
2 wiggle eyes 3mm
2" heavy Black thread
Fabri-Tac Glue

INSTRUCTIONS:
• Cut out body from foam using pattern.
• Cut 2 sets of wings from tulle.
• Knot sets of wings together.
• Glue the pom pom to the eraser end of the pencil.
• Glue foam body to the pom pom.
• Cut thread in half and stiffen the pieces with glue. Glue to the back of the ¾" Black pom pom for antennae. Glue eyes to head. Glue head to foam body and Yellow pom pom.
• Glue stripe and wings to body.

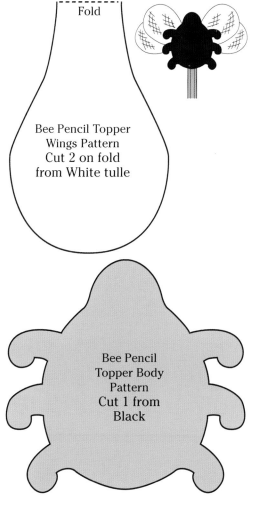

Fold

Bee Pencil Topper Wings Pattern
Cut 2 on fold from White tulle

Bee Pencil Topper Body Pattern
Cut 1 from Black

Cat Head Pattern

Tail Pattern

Paws Pattern

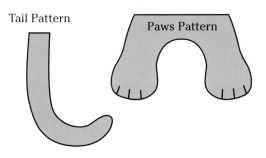

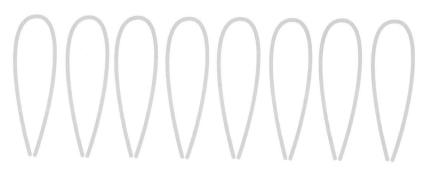

Sunflower Petal Pattern
Make 16

Sunflower

You don't need a special occasion to make something special. Give a sunny flower for Mom or Grandma just because...

SIZE: 5" x 10"

MATERIALS:
Styrofoam balls (one 3", one 2")
Dark Chocolate acrylic paint
52 wiggle eyes 7mm
Chenille stems (4 Gold, 3 Forest Green)
8" dowel $^3/16$" diameter
$2^1/2$" clay pot
24" of Gold $^5/8$" ribbon
Spanish moss
Paintbrush
Kids Choice Glue!

INSTRUCTIONS:
• Cut 3" ball in half and paint Dark Chocolate.
• Cut each Gold chenille stem into 4 even pieces.
• Form a petal shape with each piece.
• Dip ends into glue and push evenly around cut edge of ball.
• Wrap 3 Green chenille stems around dowel pulling out 2 leaves between coils.
• Glue top end of dowel and push into flower.
• Glue wiggle eyes to face of flower.
• Glue 2" ball into bottom of clay pot.
• Glue end of dowel and push into ball. Let dry.
• Cover ball with Spanish moss.
• Glue ribbon around rim of pot and tie bow.

Flower Mirror

Hot pink and sunny yellow surround your reflection with bright color and fun shapes.

SIZE: 12½" x 12½"

MATERIALS:
Styrofoam 5⅞" disc
3" round mirror
Chenille stems (9 Yellow, 16 Light Pink, 8 Medium Pink, 10 Dark Pink, 1 White)
Lemon Yellow acrylic paint
Paintbrush
Fabri-Tac or Kids Choice Glue!

INSTRUCTIONS:
• Paint disc Lemon Yellow. Let dry.
• Glue mirror to center of disc.
• Spiral 9 Yellow stems.
• Glue around mirror.
• Spiral Light Pink stem dotting glue to hold.
• Bend second Light Pink stem in half forming point.
• Wrap around spiral, dotting glue to edges.
• Repeat with Medium Pink and Dark Pink stems.
• Join all ends together, dip in glue, and push into side of disc.
• Make 7 more petals and evenly push into disc.
• Wrap 2 Dark Pink stems around disk in front of petals. Trim ends.
• Cut 4" of White stem and push into back of disc as a hanger.

Yellow Spiral Pattern Make 9

Pink Flower Petal Spiral Pattern Make 8

Sunflower Stem and Leaves Pattern

Wrap a Green stem around a dowel.

Letter B

SIZE: $8\frac{1}{2}$" x $9\frac{1}{2}$"

MATERIALS:
$9\frac{1}{2}$" wooden letter B
Acrylic paints (Baby Blue, White Wash)
$\frac{1}{2}$" pom poms (8 Red, 2 White, 1 Black)
$\frac{3}{4}$" pom poms (1 Black, 2 Yellow)
1" pom poms (3 Yellow, 2 White)
4 Black 5mm pom poms
Chenille stems
    (Green, Black, Silver glitter)
Paintbrush
Fabri-Tac Glue

INSTRUCTIONS:

Letter:
• Paint letter Baby Blue.
• Crumble paper towel and dip into White Wash.
• Dot onto Blue letter. Let dry.

Flower:
• Cut 9" of Green stem.
• Bend 2 leaves on bottom leaving the remainder straight.
• Glue to letter.
• Glue 1" Yellow pom pom in center of flower.
• Glue 8 Red pom poms around Yellow.

Large Bee:
• Glue two 1" Yellow pom poms together.
• Wrap 8" of Black stem around Yellow body.
• Glue $\frac{3}{4}$" Black pom pom as head and two 1" White pom poms for wings.
• Cut $1\frac{1}{2}$" of Silver stem, fold into V, and glue to head.
• Glue 2 small Black pom poms to ends.
• Glue bee to letter.
• Repeat for small bee using two $\frac{3}{4}$" Yellow pom poms for body, $\frac{1}{2}$" Black for head, and $\frac{1}{2}$" White for wings.

Everybody loves to see their initial decorating their personal spaces. Make this pretty project for your bedroom wall or locker.

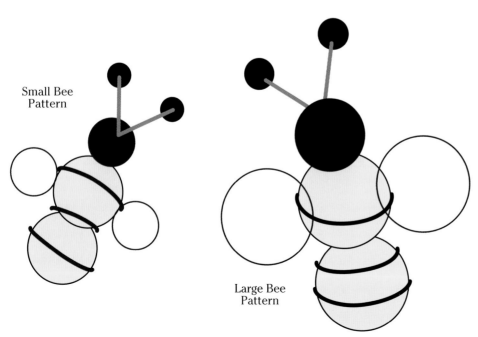

Small Bee Pattern

Large Bee Pattern

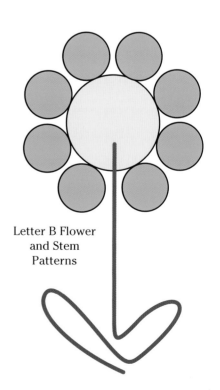

Letter B Flower and Stem Patterns

Hairband

You have eyes on the top of your head. Playful and unique, everyone will want to see this!

SIZE: 15"

MATERIALS:
Blue cloth hairband
4 wiggle eyes 15mm
6 wiggle eyes 12mm
9 wiggle eyes 7mm
12 wiggle eyes 5mm
Kids Choice Glue!

INSTRUCTIONS:
• Begin gluing eyes to center of hairband.
• Randomly glue eyes $2^1/2$" down both sides.

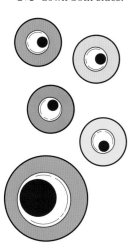

Oval Wiggle Eyes Frame

Show off your favorite photo in a fun frame that is so easy to make! Remember this project when Mother's Day and Father's Day come around - it's a great gift for Mom or Dad.

SIZE: $6^1/2$" x $8^1/2$"

MATERIALS:
4" x 6" oval frame
Wiggle eyes (13 eyes 7mm, 17 eyes 12mm, 18 eyes 15mm)
White Wash acrylic paint
Circle punches ($^1/2$", $^7/8$")
Cardstock (Blue, Green, Red, Yellow, Orange)
24" of Black and White dotted $^3/8$" wide ribbon
Paintbrush
Kids Choice Glue!

INSTRUCTIONS
• Paint oval frame White Wash.
• Punch eighteen $^1/2$" and eighteen $^7/8$" circles from colored cardstock.
• Adhere circles to frame randomly.
• Glue 15mm and 12mm eyes to colored circles.
• Glue 7mm eyes to frame.
• Glue ribbon around outside edge of frame.

Little Chick

Cuddly and cute, this chick makes an adorable decoration for your Easter basket.

SIZE: 2½" x 3½"

MATERIALS:
Yellow pom poms (one 2½", one 1½")
2" x 2" Orange felt
2 wiggle eyes 7mm
Fabri-Tac Glue

INSTRUCTIONS:
• Cut out feet and beak from felt.
• Glue the pom poms together.
• Glue the eyes, beak and feet in place.

Foot
Cut 2

Double Beak
Cut 1

With a checker-board shell, this turtle is bound to win. Make this cheery character to decorate your window or book shelf.

Diagram of each spiral piece formed into rectangles

Wrap 3 Dark Green stems around a ball begining under the spirals.

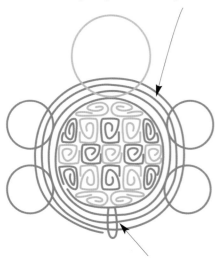

Cut and fold a 2" stem in half, insert it in the end as a tail.

Turtle

SIZE: 4½" x 5"

MATERIALS:
1 Styrofoam 3" ball
4 Green 1" pom poms
1 Light Green 1½" pom pom
Chenille stems (2 Dark Green,
    3 Lime, 4 Green)
2 wiggle eyes 7mm
Fabri-Tac Glue

INSTRUCTIONS:
• Cut ball in half.
• Cut Lime and Dark Green chenille stems into fourths.
• Spiral each piece squeezing to form rectangles.
• Glue 5 spirals in 3 rows on top of ball, alternating colors.
• Glue remaining 4 spirals to ends of rows.
• Cut 2" of Green stem, fold in half, and insert in end as tail.
• Use 3 Green stems to wrap around ball beginning under spirals.
• Glue head and legs to body.
• Glue eyes to head.

Fun and fuzzy critters and animals are designed as decorations and 'to touch'.

They are not intended as toys and are not suitable for children 3 years of age and under.

WARNING!
CHOKING HAZARD
Small Parts. Not for children under 3 years.

Pom Pom Kitty

Make a purr-fectly cute kitty for your room. This pretty kitty is content to sit on your bed, computer desk or window sill.

SIZE: 5" x 6"

MATERIALS:
Pom poms (3 White $2\frac{1}{2}$", 12 White 1", 2 White $\frac{3}{4}$", 1 Pink $\frac{1}{4}$")
$1\frac{1}{2}$" x 3" White felt
2 Blue 12mm cat's eye half round beads
8 Clear 7mm rhinestones
18" Blue $\frac{3}{8}$" wide ribbon
5" White jumbo chenille stem
6" Clear cat whiskers
Fabri-Tac Glue

INSTRUCTIONS:
• Glue two $2\frac{1}{2}$" pom poms together for body.
• Glue 1" pom poms in groups of 3 for legs.
• Glue legs to bottom of body.
• Glue $2\frac{1}{2}$" pom pom to top of body for head.
• Glue two $\frac{3}{4}$" pom poms on face for muzzle.
• Glue the Pink pom pom to face for nose.
• Glue eyes to face.
• Cut six 1" whiskers.
• Dip ends in glue and insert whiskers into muzzle. Trim.
• Cut ears from felt using pattern and clip in center.
• Overlap ear pleats and glue allowing ear to be concave.
• Shape tail from chenille stem and glue in back.
• Glue ears to top of head.
• Cut 7" of ribbon for collar.
• Glue rhinestones around collar $\frac{1}{2}$" apart.
• Glue collar around neck.
• Use remaining ribbon to tie a bow.
• Glue bow to tail.

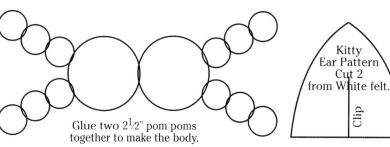

Glue two $2\frac{1}{2}$" pom poms together to make the body.

Glue three 1" pom poms together for each leg.

Kitty Ear Pattern Cut 2 from White felt.

Clip

Glue $2\frac{1}{2}$" pom pom to top for head. Glue two $\frac{3}{4}$" pom poms on face for muzzle. Glue Pink pom pom to face for nose, glue on eyes, whiskers, ears and tail.

Bunny

Hop into a creative and cute project with this sweet bunny.

SIZE: 4" x 5½"

MATERIALS:
  Styrofoam 2½" ball
  Pom poms (2 White 2", 2 White 1½", 7 White 1",
    4 White ¾", 2 White ½", 1 Pink ½", 6 Pink ¼")
  Chenille stems (Orange, Green)
  8" of ribbon
  2 wiggle eyes 7mm
  Fiberfill
  Fabri-Tac Glue

INSTRUCTIONS:
• Cut ball in half.
• Glue fiberfill to lower half.
• Glue 2" White pom pom to ball.
• Glue second 2" pom pom to top of first.
• On head, glue 2 White ¾" and ½" Pink pom poms as cheeks and nose.
• Glue eyes.
• For each ear glue two 1", one ¾", and one ½" White pom poms.
• Glue 2 White 1½" pom poms to body as feet.
• Glue 3 Pink ¼" pom poms to each foot.
• Glue 2 White 1" pom poms to body as hands and one 1" as tail.
• Tie ribbon around neck and make bow.
• Spiral 5" piece of Orange stem into carrot by squeezing one end to a point.
• Fold 2" piece of Green stem into V and glue to back of carrot.
• Glue point of carrot in bunny's mouth.

*What's up, Doc?
Hop into a creative
and cute project with
this sweet bunny.*

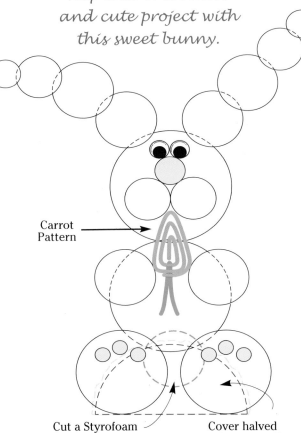

Carrot
Pattern →

Cut a Styrofoam
Ball in half

Cover halved
Styrofoam ball
with Fiberfill

Bumble Bee

Share the buzz with your friends and have fun making a hive of these busy bees.

SIZE: 5" x 6"

MATERIALS:
Pom poms (3 Black 1", 1 Yellow 1", 1 Yellow ¾")
12mm Chenille stems (1 Black 18", 1 White 9")

INSTRUCTIONS:
Antennae:
• Cut 4" of Black stem.
• Fold in half and shape into antennae.
Legs:
• Cut stems 4", 5" and 5½".
Body:
• Glue pom poms together as shown in diagram.
• Glue antennae to head.
• Fold each leg stem in half and wrap around the body.
• Shape legs.
Wings:
• Fold White stem in half and wrap around body.
• Shape each wing and wrap the end around the center of the body.

**WARNING!
CHOKING HAZARD**
Small Parts. Not for children under 3 years.

Fun and Fuzzy Animals

Lamb

Counting sheep just got easier. Make this lovable lamb for your nightstand or bedroom dresser.

SIZE: 4½" x 7"

MATERIALS:
Styrofoam 4" egg
86 White ¾" pom poms
1 Black 2" pom pom
1 Pink ½" pom pom
2 wiggle eyes 7mm
Chenille stems (5 Black, 1 White)
Dowel ³⁄16" diameter
8" of Blue ¼" wide ribbon
Fabri-Tac Glue

INSTRUCTIONS:
• Cut dowel into four 3" pieces using scissors.
• Wrap each with 1 Black chenille stem.
• Push into bottom of egg as legs.
• Glue Black pom pom on small end of egg as head.
• Glue all White pom poms to body.
• Glue Pink pom pom and wiggle eyes to head.
• Cut two 2" pieces of Black stem, fold in half, and glue to head as ears.
• Cut 2" of White stem, fold and glue to back as tail.
• Make bow from ribbon and glue to neck.

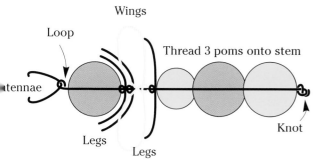

Wings

Loop

Antennae

Legs

Legs

Thread 3 poms onto stem

Knot

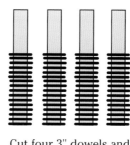

Cut four 3" dowels and wrap each with 1 Black stem for legs.

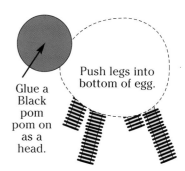

Glue a Black pom pom on as a head.

Push legs into bottom of egg.

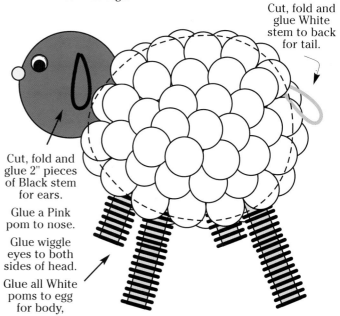

Cut, fold and glue White stem to back for tail.

Cut, fold and glue 2" pieces of Black stem for ears.

Glue a Pink pom to nose.

Glue wiggle eyes to both sides of head.

Glue all White poms to egg for body,

St. Nick

He's chubby and plump, a fun and jolly old elf. Make your holiday bright with a cheery Santa.

SIZE: 3" x 5½"

MATERIALS:

Pom poms (1 Red 3", 1 Pink 1½", 2 Black 1", 31 White ½", 8 White ¼", 1 Pink ¼")

3" x 3" Red felt

2 wiggle eyes 5mm

¼" Gold jingle bell

2½" of Red and White chenille stem

Fabri-Tac Glue

INSTRUCTIONS:

- Glue Red and Pink pom poms together for head and body.
- Glue ½" pom poms around face as shown.
- Glue Pink pom pom to face for nose.
- Glue eyes in place.
- Glue Black pom poms to bottom for gloves.
- Glue four ¼" pom poms around each glove.
- Twist chenille stems together and bend into a candy cane.
- Glue candy cane to glove.
- Cut out felt hat using pattern.
- Fold on the lines, and glue the overlap at the back.
- Glue hat to head.
- Glue jingle bell to end of hat.
- Glue end of hat to side of head as shown.

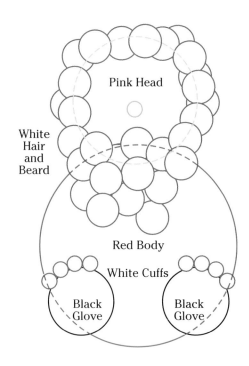

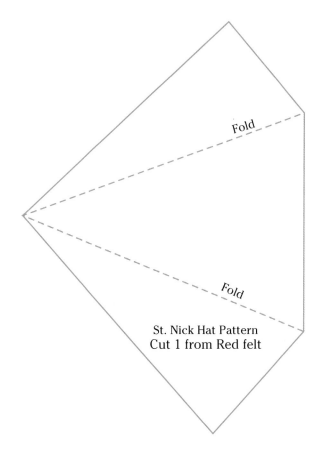

St. Nick Hat Pattern
Cut 1 from Red felt

**WARNING!
CHOKING HAZARD**

Small Parts. Not for children under 3 years.

Teddy Bear

Cuddly and cute any time of the year, this teddy with his holiday bow is all ready for Santa to arrive.

SIZE: 5" x 6"

MATERIALS:
Pom poms (2 Tan 3", 7 Tan 2", 1 Tan 1")
3 Black 10mm half round beads
Ribbon (18" Plaid $5/8$" wide, 3" Red $1/8$" wide)
$1\frac{1}{2}$" x 4" cardstock
Markers (Red, Green)
$1/8$" hole punch
Fabri-Tac Glue

INSTRUCTIONS:
• Glue 3" pom poms together for head and body.
• Glue 2" pom poms for arms, legs, ears and tail.
• Glue 1" pom pom to face for muzzle.
• Glue beads for eyes and nose.
• Tie Plaid ribbon in a bow around the neck.
• Fold cardstock in half and write "Merry Xmas".
• Decorate card edge with markers.
• Punch a hole in the card corner and tie to neck ribbon.

Reindeer Candy Cane

Stuff your family stockings or make our Rudolph as a favor for your holiday celebration.

SIZE: $2\frac{1}{2}$" x 9"

MATERIALS:
Candy cane
Brown chenille stem
Red $\frac{1}{4}$" pom pom
2 wiggle eyes 7mm
12" of Green $\frac{3}{4}$" wide ribbon
Kids Choice Glue!

INSTRUCTIONS:
• Wrap center of Brown stem around hook of candy cane.
• Bend into antlers.
• Glue eyes and pom pom nose to hook.
• Wrap ribbon around reindeer's neck and tie into bow.
• Trim the ends.

Holiday Animals

You'll love every fuzzy character and critter.
Hang them on your tree as ornaments or just
enjoy making each one.

Necklace

Touchably soft, fuzzy and light - make this necklace in your favorite colors.

SIZE: 25"

MATERIALS:
28" Black yarn
Nine ³⁄₄" pom poms
(Maroon, Green, Blue, Red, Black)
4 Purple chenille stems
2 drinking straws
Large eye needle

INSTRUCTIONS:
• Cut chenille stems in half.
• Wrap each piece around drinking straw.
• Push stem to end of straw and cut straw.
• Make 8 chenille beads.
• Thread needle with yarn.
• To make threading easier, wrap end of yarn with piece of masking tape.
• Push needle through one pom pom and one bead.
• Repeat until all are threaded on yarn.
• Knot yarn and trim.

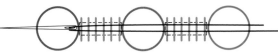

Cut chenille stems in half and wrap each piece around a drinking straw to make beads. Push a needle threaded with yarn through one pom pom and one bead. Repeat this process until all are threaded on yarn.

Jewelry & Bag

It's easy to make colorful wearables!

Black Bracelet

Make party favors that your friends will enjoy - without spending a lot of money. This bracelet is made from an empty potato chip can. What a way to recycle!

SIZE: 1¹⁄₂" x 10"

MATERIALS:
1¹⁄₂" ring cut from a Pringles™ potato chip can
10" of Black 1¹⁄₂" wide ribbon
Chenille stems (3 Orange, 1 Pink, 1 Turquoise)
8 Turquoise 5mm pom poms
Craft scissors
Fabri-Tac Glue

INSTRUCTIONS:
• Cut a 1¹⁄₂" ring from a potato chip can.
• Cover the ring with Black ribbon.
• Braid 1 Orange, 1 Turquoise, and 1 Pink stem together.
• Glue to center of bracelet.
• Cut 2 Orange stems in fourths.
• Spiral each piece, glue evenly around bracelet.
• Glue pom poms to spirals.

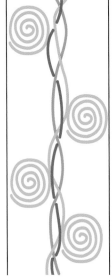

Spiral and
Braiding Pattern

Beach Bag

This summer, tote your gear to the beach or pool in style with a bag that's easy to identify as your own.

SIZE: 13" x 14"

MATERIALS:
13" x 14" Light Blue canvas tote
Blue Chiffon acrylic paint
Plaid Simply Stamps Jive Alphabet
1" pom poms (1 Orange, 12 Light Blue)
1½" pom poms (Lime, Turquoise)
5mm pom poms (6 Red, 7 White)
Chenille stems (1 Lime, 1 Turquoise, 1 Orange, 3 Green)
Wiggle eyes (one 3mm, two 6mm)
Paintbrush
Fabri-Tac Glue

INSTRUCTIONS:
• Paint foam letter stamps Blue Chiffon and firmly press onto tote spelling "BEACH BAG". Let dry.
• Glue Blue pom poms across top of tote.
• Wrap Green stems around paintbrush and pull coils out slightly.
• Glue to right side of bag as sea plants.
• Cut 6" of Lime stem and form fish tail.
• Cut two 3" pieces of Lime stem and form 2 fins.
• Glue fins and tail to back of large Lime pom pom and glue to tote.
• Glue 6mm eye and 2 small Red pom poms as lips to face.
• Repeat to make Turquoise fish.
• Make smaller Orange tail and glue to back of 1" Orange pom pom.
• Cut 2" of Orange stem, fold into V, and glue to back of fish as fins.
• Glue Red pom poms as lips and 3mm eye to face.
• Glue 2 or 3 White pom poms near fish as bubbles.

Zig Zag Bracelet

Make a fun bangle bracelet for yourself and all your friends. This project is quick, easy and inexpensive - great for a group activity.

SIZE: 1" x 10"

MATERIALS:
1" ring cut from a Pringles™ potato chip can
10" of White 1" wide ribbon
Chenille stems (2 Purple, 1 Dark Pink)
5mm pom poms (6 each of Turquoise, Lime, Yellow)
Fabri-Tac Glue

INSTRUCTIONS:
• Cut a 1" ring from a potato chip can.
• Cover cut piece of can with White ribbon.
• Glue Purple stems to outside edge of bracelet.
• Zigzag Pink stem, folding every 1".
• Stretch out stem until it fits around bracelet.
• Glue between Purple stems.
• Glue pom poms in empty spaces alternating colors.

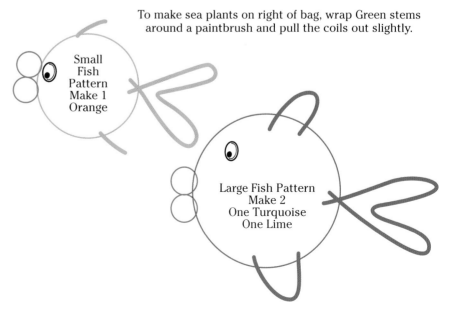

To make sea plants on right of bag, wrap Green stems around a paintbrush and pull the coils out slightly.

Small Fish Pattern Make 1 Orange

Large Fish Pattern Make 2 One Turquoise One Lime

White Cap

Shade your eyes with unique style. Create a cap in your favorite colors.

Sun Pattern for cap

MATERIALS:
White baseball cap
Chenille stems (2 Yellow,
    1 Dark Pink, 1 Pink,
    1 Lavender, 1 Green)
$3/4$" pom poms (Yellow, Purple)
$1/2$" Dark Pink pom pom
Fabri-Tac Glue

INSTRUCTIONS:
• Spiral 1 Yellow stem.
• Zigzag 1 Yellow stem making 7 points.
• Glue zigzag to back of spiral and glue to top left of hat as sun.
• Zigzag Dark Pink stem to form five 1" points.
• Zigzag Pink stem to form five $3/4$" points
• Zigzag Lavender to form five $1/2$" points.
• Join ends forming flowers.
• Glue flowers to hat.
• Glue Yellow pom pom to center of Dark Pink flower, Purple to Pink flower, and Pink to Lavender flower.
• Cut three 2" pieces of Green stem and fold in half forming leaves.
• Glue one to each flower.

Pink Flower and Leaf patterns for cap

Create cute and sassy wearables with caps and shoes in cheerful colors!

Shoes

Don't settle for plain white! Step out in style with sneakers you decorate yourself.

MATERIALS:
White canvas sneakers
Chenille stems (3 Dark Pink, 1 Yellow, 1 Purple, 1 Green)
2 Yellow $1/2$" pom poms
2 drinking straws
Fabri-Tac Glue

INSTRUCTIONS:
• Cut Yellow, Pink, and Purple stems in half.
• Coil one piece around straw.
• Push coil to end of straw and cut straw.
• Repeat for remaining pieces.
• Untie shoelaces and thread each chenille bead onto laces.
• Zigzag 2 Dark Pink stems forming five $3/4$" points.
• Glue one to each sneaker.
• Glue pom pom to centers of flowers.
• Cut four 2" pieces of Green stem and fold in half forming leaves.
• Glue 2 to each flower.

Shoe Pattern
Wrap a straw with chenille.